P.I.M.P.

Perception. Influence. Marketing. Presentation.

By: Infanit Percent

This book is based on a true story seen and told through the eyes of the author. Names have been changed to protect the innocent but any likenesses in names, places, businesses etc. are a direct result of parts played in the life of the author.

Copyright 2018 by Bernard Lofton

All rights reserved, including the right to reproduce this book or portions thereof in any form whatsoever.

Acknowledgements

I would like to give a special thanks to my parents, relatives and friends because without y'all there wouldn't be a me. Without y'all, I wouldn't have the experiences and insight that I have to this day.

Also, I want to give a thanks to the lovely, Justjae Warner for her help in putting together this book on my behalf.

Table of Contents

CHAPTER ONE   3

CHAPTER TWO   16

CHAPTER THREE   26

CHAPTER FOUR   25

Prologue...

On November 19, 1988, Tisha Wooden gave birth to me. I was given my father's name. However, my father's name was Bernard Alexander Lofton whereas my name was Bernard Alexander Wooden.

When I was in elementary school, my father went and signed my birth certificate. His intention was to make me a junior, but it didn't happen like that. Instead, I ended up with two last names. So, my name was and is Bernard Alexander Wooden Lofton.

I'm also known as Poo, P.Hundred, Hunnn Dunn but mostly recently and pertaining to my books...I am known as Infanit Percent. The title of this book is P.I.M.P.

When I hear the word pimp, I think about hoes, bitches, tricks and money being made and given to a person or an overseer. I was also reflecting on when I read the book <u>PIMP</u> by *Iceberg Slim* in which he breaks down his memoirs and life stories as a world-renowned pimp who was mentored by Sweet Jones.

However, this book is about pimping the system for the good and positive cause. No names will be mentioned, this ain't no book based on dry snitching. However, I will use my life to illustrate the four points. We break down P.I.M.P as an acronym which is *Perception, Influence, Marketing* and *Presentation*.

CHAPTER ONE
PERCEPTION

Perception is the ability to see, hear or become aware of something through the senses

The oldest memory of my pops is this. I recall us being in a dropped top car when I was a little baby. I only had on a t-shirt and a pamper. He was driving with three friends in the car.

I remember them passing me around in the car, kind of like that scene in south central when OG Bobby Johnson had his baby in the car with them.

Since I was little, I always had problems with my eyes. I remember my mother telling me that I sat too close to the TV and that must have messed up my eyes. I'm nearsighted, meaning objects further away get blurry to me.

The crazy thing about growing up is that I really didn't get corrections for my eyes as far as glasses or contacts until later on in middle school. It wasn't that we couldn't afford it, it was more so because I chose to go without them or felt like I didn't need them.

I remember one particular incident that made me always where my corrections for my eyes, whether that be contacts or my glasses. I went to this track meet at Hugh Mills Stadium with a friend of the hood. At that time, I wasn't wearing my glasses even though I needed them. I walked up to a guy that I perceived to be my best friend (yes, I was that blind), but as I got closer to the guy, I realized that he wasn't June. As I was realizing who he wasn't, he realized who I was. It was like seeing me triggered a memory in his mind. Basically, we had gotten into it with some guys from the eastside of Albany two weekends ago. I happened to be one of the guys in the commotion at that club and it triggered that memory when he saw me.

So, he and his guys tried to surround me and the guy I walked in with walked away and left me. A girl that I went to middle school with saved me, she jumped in the middle of the group like, "y'all ain't finna jump on him."

So, I ended up leaving the game, walking around the stadium and going back into the neighborhood. My hood was walking distance from the stadium that every high school played football or had a track meet at in the city.

Upon walking around the stadium, I see a truck with ten guys on the bed of the truck and maybe three guys inside. They pulled in front of me and jumped out. All I was able to do was run, because I wasn't wearing no type of glasses at this time. I couldn't see to know if they had guns, bats or chains or whatever. I wasn't trying to be wearing any black eyes or knots on my face.

In the process of running to the hood, I could have sworn I heard some of the guys running behind me. They were closing in on me. I don't know how I missed it, but by the grace of God I was able to jump through a clothesline fence. Some of the guys that were chasing me tripped over the fence.

So, I made it back to the neighborhood and told some of my guys what had happened and they immediately jumped in cars and vehicles to go check the seen out while I sat on the porch and caught my breath.

While I was catching my breath, my cousin came and sat with me and he told me something that stuck with me to this day. He said, "You see, this gang shit ain't no joke. It ain't no type of life or living to have to constantly have to look over your shoulder."

With that being said, I always give respect and strive to be prepared because you never know what's going to happen. So, the crazy thing about that situation was that a lot of my guys and I, had planned to make a grand entrance at the next event or game the following weekend. In the meantime, I went to a scrimmage game at Albany High School during the week. When

I walked inside this game by myself, I saw three guys get up and leave. When they left one of my friends from the school walked in and asked me if I knew those guys. I said that I had never seen them before.

Come to find out they were some of the guys that had been chasing me and they told him that they were going to get the hell on because they thought I was about to do some type of retaliation. Like I said, I couldn't see, I didn't know who all were chasing me. I just remembered the guy that I mistook for my friend.

A couple of days later, another game happened and that's when we went to war with the whole Dougherty High track team. That was a crazy night.

I remember my first-time smoking weed. One of my cousins had tried to blow me a shotgun…that's when you hold your mouth over the fireside of the blunt and blow the smoke out to the next person and they inhale it all in. The crazy thing about this experience was that when my cousin was blowing the smoke into my mouth, I actually put my lips on the blunt. Immediately he was like, "cuz that ain't how it's supposed to be done. They began joking and teasing me.

So, when I got home... I was high as hell. My mother asked to smell my hand. When she did, she smelled weed of course. So, she tried to whoop me, then called my father.

My father came to the house the next day. He whooped the hell out of me. Told me to bend over the bed…I wanted to buck up at him. I wanted to raise hell because in that moment I felt like he was a stranger even though I knew him all my life.

After the whooping, I stormed out the back door, no telling where I was going. I was just trying to get away.

My father said, "Come here, son. Come ride with me." He took me to the cemetery and started talking about death and people dying. He showed me a few relatives' graves and gave me the reasons why they died.

All the while, I'm thinking *what the hell. Why am I at the cemetery. What are you trying to show me or what's the purpose of this?*

As we left, we got in the car and he immediately pulled a bag of weed from under the seat and blunt and said, "Roll up, young buck."

I looked at him crazy thinking, *didn't you just whoop me for this shit?* At that moment all we could do was laugh. It was so crazy to me.

What he told me was that he would rather me smoke with him as opposed to smoking with anyone else because other people put extra stuff in the weed that they smoke. That was what he told me and also that he had to make it look good for my mother.

Ever since that moment, I looked at my father in a different light. I knew him before but since that moment, I started to revere him. I began to look at him like my hero and I was able to open up to him more after that moment.

My take on perception is this. People perceive what you show them. In the midst of almost getting jumped, the people that were in the scrimmage game and walked out still perceived me to be some type of threat. They left the game in the beginning of the game because of what they thought I was going to do.

In business, perception is always key. When people perceive you to be a trustworthy businessman or just a trustworthy individual then they will be more receptive to do business with you.

Perception is important in business, in relationships and in life in general because if you are perceived to people as being weak…you will get walked all over. Nobody will ever take you seriously if they perceive you as inferior. If you want to be taken seriously, the perception of who you are has to reign true within your demonstration, within your life, and within your livelihood.

CHAPTER TWO
INFLUENCE

Influence is the capacity to have an effect on the character, development, or behavior of someone of something.

I remember another ass whooping that my pops gave me. In middle school, me and my second oldest brother Shrije had both moved in with our father. We were staying on the southside in Albany at that time.

To me… I was treated different. Yes, I was the oldest, but I felt like I wasn't getting the attention I desired. I felt like I was being treated different in comparison to my dad's children of the woman that he married.

So, one particular day, I was just fed up. Pops came in the house and asked why the dishes weren't washed or something to that extent and I just raised hell or let it all go. I said something along the lines of, "I ain't finna do this…" The next thing I know, I was getting another ass whooping.

At that moment, I packed up my stuff and called my mother. I was ready to move back with her. A little later, Pops called me back into the dining room and said, "What's going on? Talk to me."

I tried to open my mouth and let him know how I was feeling but I couldn't get the words out of my mouth.

Pops then said, "If you can't say it, write it down." I felt relieved because although I couldn't say it, it was easy for me to write it all down.

Once I wrote it down, I gave him the piece of paper and he read it. Then we started having a different conversation. From that moment on, I knew the power of the pen. That skill would later become vital in my life because I never dealt with emotions on my sleeves. Being able to write down what I was feeling on a sheet of paper opened up a door for me to want to write stuff down.

CME, that was what we called our neighborhood. Some people said, Crime Murder Execution…others said Collect Money Every day. Either way we called it CME. In my high school I became like a menace to society in one aspect of my life. Although I was making honor roll and keeping perfect attendance in school…in the streets I was still doing a lot of treacherous and crazy shit.

We used to love fighting, we used to destroy properties, and we used to cause so much destruction in our community.

There were a lot of us in the groups when we would destroy something, so the brotherhood feeling was what enticed me the most. I loved being connected with brothers and sisters all across the city. No matter if you were on the north south east or west, if you were under that black and gold bandana… you were considered a brother or a sister and we showed that love and respect for one another.

I wanted to become a major influence in my community. Although we were organized doing a lot of negative deeds, I still saw myself branching off and doing something positive.

A lot of people in my neighborhood were aware of me being smart, so I was an image to a lot of the youth coming up under me in my community that you can be street smart and book smart and nobody will mess with you. I was proud to be that character in that regards because prior to that, when you look at TV or any type of media… it portrays the smart guy getting bullied or picked on. That wasn't the case in my situation, I was a smart guy and, in some aspects, I was a bully too…but I was fair.

Then one day, all hell broke loose. Earlier this particular day, the year was 2005…one of the homies from the hood had gotten into it with another individual at the school. Like always, we settled disputes by fighting. This particular fight took place behind my house. It was a crowd of maybe 50 or 100 of us.

Needless to say, after the fight between those two jumped off, some of the homies jumped on these guys.

So, the police were called and the larger crowd dispersed. It ended up breaking into three crowds. I was in the crowd walking way in the back, but my little brother Boola was in the first crowd which the police happened to stop and ask a few questions.

There was one officer named Officer Jones. Everybody in the hood knew who he was, a lot of times ones used to curse him out…talk shit with him…laugh and joke with him. This particular day, he had a white partner with him and my brother proceeded to joke and laugh with him, but he was met with a different attitude than usual. The police ended up jumping on my brother, but instead of taking him to jail, they ended up bringing him to our house.

By this time everybody at the house had gotten wind of what happened and we were on our way to the precinct when we saw them pull up to our house. My mother began asking one of the officers for their supervisor's name and contact information because we knew they were in the wrong for what they did.

My mother's questions were met with hostility and rage, to the point where they began getting aggressive with her. A few of the officers had surrounded her as she began to make a call to the precinct and at that point they rushed her.

All I heard was my mother say, "Get this motherfucker." Next thing I know I was swinging left and right. I had knocked out two of the officers and somehow ended up in a circle fighting another. I promise you not, in that circle I was fighting a Chinese officer and I was giving it to him. I was beating him down. There were other officers making a circle around us and some of our guys were in the circle as well.

That was just crazy. Still to this day, I'm thankful because if we had been in this present time... I would be an Eric Gardner or Mike Brown. I truly believe they would have shot me down. So, I'm truly thankful to be here today and able to share my story with you in this book.

I got three points of submission that I consider my solidification of my faith. I had just moved to Atlanta and I was living with my mother. I remember praying and submitting to the Most High because I wanted to tap into the spiritual world...to be more spiritual. At this point, I had my locs and I was coming into a lot of knowledge and I wanted to be enlightened. So, I prayed for discernment and strength to carry the load that was being put on my plate. In the midst of doing that I felt myself being raised to the moon. I was looking down from the moon as if I was standing on the moon. Then, it humbled me and dropped me down to the ground. After that, I didn't know what I was supposed to be doing. I didn't know what my role in life was, I was still trying to figure it all out.

My very first job was at a warehouse by the name of ABX-Air. Eventually this company was bought by DHL. That was my first time being laid off like that.

One particular day I was going to work in a car that had faulty brakes. On my way getting off the exit, the brakes gave out on me and I ended up crashing into another car and knocking that car across the road. Upon impact, my car doors locked up immediately. I felt myself outside of my body, watching the accident happen.

So, after what felt like an eternity, the doors unlocked and I was able to get out of the car without a scratch. When I got out and looked at the car, the engine was almost into the trunk. To this day, I feel saved and blessed that I made it out of that incident without a scratch.

Fast forward back to the accident, it just so happened that the lady that I hit was a coworker from my job. Upon going to court, they ended up dropping all the charges that were against me. All in all, I know it was three tickets that were written, speeding, following too close and something else but all three were dismissed because the officers didn't show up.

The last point of the three that solidified my faith is this. I was walking to the store from leaving the hotel room and was immediately stopped by a police officer in Riverdale, Ga. Basically, the officer told me to get into the back seat of his cruiser without asking me for my name. Without reading me any types of rights. So, I was confrontational in my words as to why was I needing to be inside the back of his car.

The next thing I knew, the officer (a young, white guy) grabbed me and slammed me against the window of his car. In the midst of him doing that, I hear him get on to his radio and say, "I need back up. Resisting arrest." All the while, I'm looking at this guy like are you serious? I wasn't resisting no arrest. I didn't even know I was under arrest. At that moment I had an out of body experience in that it felt like I was a witness to my own assault.

Other police arrived at the scene and come to find out I did have a hit and run warrant out for my arrest which messed me up in that particular fight as it relates to filing for a lawsuit. They would have countersued saying that that happened because I was showing signs of being guilty.

I remember the hit and run like it was yesterday. We were at school, the Art Institute of Atlanta. A former classmate and I had agreed to match a blunt which meant that he would smoke one and I would smoke one. So, I rolled up my blunt and I figured that he had rolled up his as well. He had another classmate that let us hotbox in her car. I don't know how or why, but somehow, I ended up with the keys and we drove the car from one parking lot to another. In the process of smoking and conversing about life and stuff, it was almost time to go back to class. I had smoked my blunt and now I'm looking at the guy like... where your weed at. In the process of going back to class, I wasn't paying attention as I was backing up so I hit another car. It knocked her bumper off and left some red paint the other car.

We get back to class and I thought everything had died down...of course it didn't. They ended up having to tow her car and I ended up with a warrant.

At that time, I was already on probation in Clayton County and the situation with the police officer jumping on me was a new charge. So, that violated my probation. I also had an open case for the situation with the hit and run. So, long story short I ended up doing three months in Clayton County and a week in Sandy Springs jail.

In those three months, I read a lot. I read three different Bibles cover to cover and got multiple and different understandings from each book. I firmly believe that each version of the Bible reads different than the other. I also believe that the Bible is a book of influence, that's what I got from it. Look at all the world's religions that come from this single book.

My take on influence is this. It stems from having a following. Is your following righteous or is it unrighteous? Do ones believe in this enough to die for it, or not at all. When we look at influence, we look at the effect something or someone has on another person's life.

As for my own life and the research and insight I've been blessed with, I am a person of influence. I would like and I strive to influence the people that are looking up to me on a righteous and positive path and I will continue to do that until I am being carried by six.

CHAPTER THREE

MARKETING

Marketing: The action or business of promoting and selling products or services.

Like I mentioned when I was in jail, I did a lot of reading. In reading a lot of these books, it inspired me to want to write my own book.

I started a series of book. The first was called Mind Dread, the second was called Traveling Time. Later on when I got out, I wrote the final part and I put those three pieces together. I named the book The Life of Domino Jacobs.

I didn't really take the process as serious as I should. My only goal in writing a book at that time was just because I felt like I could do it. So, I did it.

My two favorite artists to this day are still Bob Marley and Tupac. If you look at the track record of both of those individuals, neither one got too much radio play but both had sold out shows, sold out albums and had a movement within their music and outside of their music. For instance, Bob Marley had the Rastafari culture and religion. Tupac Shakur had THUGLIFE and THE OUTLAWZ.

I studied those guys and once I realized that I wanted to take my music to the next level, I decided to do what they did which was fashion a movement behind my music.

However, it didn't go like I wanted it to go. I was always juggling different business venture, ideas and concepts to get by until that dream pans itself out or until it came into fruition with the right people.

I then reflected on business as a whole. In business you have to have a persona or target audience. Who are you potentially trying to sell to? Who do you really want to solely seek the benefits of what you have to offer?

For me, I chose myself as that persona and I created a blueprint on how to market to myself with the extent of my universal self. I looked at the world low and beyond...what is one thing that no matter where you go or where you travel to...it will be prevalent in that location. I thought long and hard on that concept because I wanted to be universal. I wanted to do business everywhere, on an international level. What came to my mind is the Bible. You can find the Bible in China, Japan, Canada, America, South Africa, South America...so forth and so on. At that moment, I began to incorporate the teachings of the Bible into my daily life, my music life and my spiritual life.

My take on marketing brings me back to a party that we threw in high school. My cousin got out of jail and we decided to throw him a coming home party. The crazy thing about this party was that we all agreed to bring something to the party which was going to be at our house which was across the street from Albany high school. Long story short, we stole everything for this party, from the food and entertainment to the beer and drinks. It was just funny how we all could have gotten locked up celebrating my cousin's homecoming.

We all enjoyed ourselves, but going back to marketing. Marketing is the promotion aspect behind what you do or what you are striving to do. The more people see the vision of what you have to offer, the more people that are going to be likely to do business with you.

I link this with that party because, even without having the means and funds to do so…if somebody believes in the cause or the vision, it ain't no telling what they are going to do behind that or for that vision.

CHAPTER FOUR
PRESENTATION

Presentation is the manner or style in which something is given, offered, or displayed.

I remember my first suit was a jean jacket suit which was given to me by my father. He later gave me another two-piece suit. The point is this, when I wear a suit...I like how it feels. It makes me feel professional and like I'm about to take care of business. That feeling made me carry myself accordingly. As a businessman, presentation is a must.

I remember at the beginning of my business career, I used to put quantity before quality. I see now that it was a mistake. Quality will always outshine and do better than a product based on quantity. Just because you have a lot of it, doesn't mean it will do well. If it's trash or if it's presented in a trash-like manner, then it won't do good. It's all about quality when you are dealing with the presentation of anything.

I was first introduced to rapping over beats in the ninth grade. One of the homies from the hood by the name of Cujo had somewhat pulled me under his wing as far as the music thing goes. To my knowledge, his brother had taught him how to rap and they had moved to Albany from Macon where they were competing in different battling competitions in different cities around the town.

What we would do was rap over beats using a tape player. On one instance we would play the music or instrumental in the background and we would hit record on the tape player to record our verses over the instrumentals. We did a whole series of mixtapes which we called Jackin for Beats.

At that point, I was inspired to do more with my music. I wanted to continue along that path of writing and spitting verses over beats. However, around that time Cujo ended up getting locked up and I was forced to continue on that path alone as far as the music goes.

Around this same time, I was put on house arrest for the fight that took place with the police. The house arrest was hosted at my father's house. I was released under my father's custody. There was a whole box monitor linked to the house phone at my father's house. Although I was now staying with my father across town, I continued to go to my same high school.

Still, I had also built a janky studio at my father's house. I use to record every night practicing my skills. I also started making my own CDs to distribute.

Later, I met a guy by the music name of Ruthless Jay. We started doing music together and came up with a group Konfidential Klick. We did a whole series of mixes and ultimately ended up completing a whole project which we later distributed on CD. Also prior to that, Jay was how I got the name P Hundred.

Before this, I was doing music and on the CDs I would right POO which was my nickname at that time. I was going by Young POO. He looked at a CD I gave him and said, "What that say, P Hundred?" From that day I did music under the name P Hundred.

We began to seek out avenues that we could possibly perform at. We really weren't successful in achieving that platform to do so in Albany because of the stigma that we felt people had towards individuals that came from the hood that we represented which was CME.

Me and Jay got into a fight over a story that I heard he was trying to disrespect my little brother and I ended up putting my hands on the brother. Still, despite that dispute, we continued to further develop the group which was Konfidential Klick.

We were still recording song after song and we also inspired people to want to do music in our hood. However, me and Jay ended up having a difference in opinion which later lead to a falling out.

We had two producers that were associated with the group. One was his cousin Slick and the other was Cap. At that time, I did not really know Cap. However, I felt ill feelings about the opportunities and beats that were given to me as oppose to those that were given to Jay. I felt that favoritism was being shown in Jay's favor because Slick was his cousin.

Once we started working on solo projects, I saw that Jay would end up with the best beats in my opinion and I would end up with what I felt were the sloppy seconds or the disregarded beats. After months of feeling that way, I ended up leaving that situation.

During the course of the separation Jay ended up getting locked up and I ended up linking with Cap. We had a sit down and conversation. I came to the knowledge that Cap was the nephew of one of my cousin's down the line on my mother's side. We were also a part of the same tribe which was the CME family. Whereas Jay and Slick were a part of the Blood family as far as tribes go.

So, we ended up coming up with the concept to do an entertainment company. We created the movement Konfidential Entertainment. This entertainment company was founded on the grounds to educate our people on the music background as far as it relates to the development of an artist.

Even back then, we saw the knowledge and insight it took to become an independent artist. Even though being an independent artist wasn't as highly favored or so mainstreamed as it is today.

I ended up moving to Atlanta with my mother to go to college and Cap ended up staying in Albany, but we always kept in touch. I looked at his mother like my mother, he looked at my daddy like his daddy. So, the bond we still share to this day is on a whole different level. I always try my best to guide that brother with the knowledge that I came to learn and know. It's still a lot I have to learn today, but Konfidential Entertainment will always be my starting point when I look back on my business developments.

To this day, my brother and my partner Cap, or also known as CEO CAP, is still carrying the banner of Konfidential Entertainment. To me, I can't do nothing but respect and love that because that will always be a part of me.

Our logo was one of the first logos that I ever created and we still carry that to this day. I'm just humbled by the longevity and time that this movement has been able to endure.

At this present time, CEO Cap is a known DJ in the city of Albany. He has a nice promotion team and is doing a lot of positive things in the community. I will always tip my hat to that brother.

I remember when I first got into the city of Atlanta, it was a whole new world to me. It was like I had hit the reset button on my life and it was like a second start.

However, I was still missing that brotherhood and sisterhood foundation that was established in our family in Albany through that CME tribe. When I would meet brothers and sisters in Atlanta that were affiliated with certain gangs, I would always get asked questions like "Do I know such-and-such". It was amazing to me that a lot of the ones named, I did know and it was based off of their affiliation with whatever tribe that they were a part of in my hometown. So, immediately, I wanted to find an extension with my CME family.

In the beginning, I was led to believe that we were part of the Four Corner Hustler's family or the Four Corner Hustler's tribe which is also a faction of the Vice Lords' nation. I became infatuated in learning the history as it pertains to the Vice Lords. They were in proximity to some of the teachings that we shared through that CME tribe and even the colors they wore were the same in that CME family.

So, I found a second home in the Vice Lord nation before I even got legitimately in tune with the people that I needed to know. After doing my history acknowledging the movement, I was impressed with the history. The Vice Lord nation was able to get a Rockafella grant to develop a certain neighborhood and community in the city of Chicago and they had several businesses from the African Lion shop and a Tasty Freeze ice cream to a youth center for the kids. I was amazed at the develop on that level for our people and our poverty-stricken community. That inspired me.

However, I wasn't naïve to the fact that some Lords still demonstrated in a lower nature aspect of themselves and behaved in a gang-like fashion. I wasn't blind to that side of the movement, but all I knew was that I wanted to rotate with the brothers and sisters that were on that path to righteousness. I wanted to make an impact for our people on a national level and I know my heart is big and what I'm capable of. I needed a vehicle to supplement the mission of bettering our people and Vice Lords was my vehicle.

Everything is about having a vehicle. Once you got the right vehicle to move in, you can get from point A to point B on time and proficiently as possible. But you can't expect to drive all the way from Atlanta to California in a bucket. That's the same scenario as dealing with a movement for our people. The vehicle got to be right and that was my take on why I was inspired to connect and align myself with the Vice Lord nation. It was only right or it felt right to do that. Still, at that time I wasn't in tune with many people of the nation. I may have met a few in passing but I wasn't in tune.

October 2014 my little brother Boola had gotten killed in the city of Atlanta. That situation took a whole chunk out of my chest. I really didn't know what to do or how to go about living. Not necessarily saying that I was suicidal or wanted to die. It just was that a major part of my center was knocked off the rocker after hearing that my brother was killed.

Of course, I thought about retaliation. I thought about doing a whole lot of things that ultimately wouldn't bring my brother back to us. I just felt lost.

Maybe it was God, but I saw this flyer on Facebook that read: Stop the Violence and that there was a rally going on down the street in the neighborhood that I was living in at the time. The movement that was hosting this event was called POPS Movement.

Immediately, I reached out to the brother that I saw was hosting this event on Facebook. I messaged him on Facebook Messenger and asked him if it was cool if I brought my camera out to the rally and took some shots just so I could be in the vicinity of something positive. Prior to this, I never thought of myself as the type to rally or protest or march or any of those things. I considered myself more like Malcom X than Martin Luther King. I believed at that time that it was more so action in what we should be doing as opposed to asking people outside of us to do what we should be doing ourselves.

However, at this first rally, my eyes were opened. I saw a lot of different brothers and sisters coming together. Ones gave speeches and talked about the violence in the community as well as exercising a plan to combat the violence…that we should be joining hands to accomplish such a thing.

I was looking for the brother that I inboxed on Facebook to shake his hand and let him know that it was a positive demonstration, I didn't see him there. However, one of the speakers got back up towards the end of the rally and said that they were going to read a letter from the brother by the name of Hest.

In this letter, the writer expressed gratitude, support, love and blessings for the job that ones were doing and partaking in. At the end of the letter, I found out that the brother was incarcerated. It humbled me that ones on the inside could do something as beautiful as throwing a protest or really on the outside.

In that moment, it gave me a fulfilment. It filled my spirit. Finally, I found something to fill the void that my brother's passing left in my chest. After that, I took the movement onto my shoulders. I was impressed with everything from the organizing, the proficiency of the events that were put together, and to the accountability of the six-step program that was implemented through the organization.

Although everything on the inside ain't always what it seems on the outside, I still attribute a lot of my organizational skills and a lot of my people skills as it relates to helping people in our community to my joining this movement.

On my spiritual side, I also was growing and becoming more enlightened…even up to this day. When I started the path of growing my locs, I became infatuated with the Rastafari movement, culture and religion. So, I also consider myself a part of this culture, even though I didn't have any connection to being born in Jamaica or attending some type of worship pertaining to the culture or religion…like a lot of the people that are from the island. All I knew was that the spirit and energy of Bob Marley lead me to believe that this movement was the way to be or that it was the answer for me.

At that time, I did not know a whole lot about His Imperial Majesty Haile Selassie I. Instead, a lot of my early research in history stem from the teachings of The Honorable Marcus M. Garvey. I knew more about Garvey than I did about Haile

Selassie I even though I was calling myself in the name of Rastafari which was Haile Selassie I's pre-coronation name.

In 2017, all of that changed. I was introduced to the Ethiopian World Federation. Through my involvement in developing a local here in the city of Atlanta, I became abreast with all of the history and knowledge as it pertains to Haile Selassie I.

This brother knew over 17 different languages. He was the only person in the world whose lineage could be traced all the way back to King Solomon and the Queen of Sheba. Also, through this organization, I found out that the Ark of Covenant is still in Ethiopia to this day. I then became inspired to be like the Ethiopians in the aspect of how they are disciplined in their faith.

Although the media and society give us this picture of Ethiopia being this starving country and we see images like "Starvin Marvin" (who was an Ethiopian on a show called South Park) …portraying a negative and tainted image of Ethiopia…I've learned that this is not the case.

Ethiopian is the oldest Christian nation and it is the first Jewish nation. Even in the Quran, it speaks of the Prophet Muhammad PBUH seeking haven in Ethiopia to escape the bounty or assassination attempt that was placed on his life. Ultimately, he was granted refuge by the Ethiopian Emperor of that time to escape his captors and conspirators who sought to do him harm for his philosophies.

I then, find myself absorbed with the teaching and culture of this beautiful country and the continent of Africa. Ethiopia is the only country in Africa that wasn't colonized. When Africa was being colonized and stripped of its resources…what those devils did was kill the knowledgeable people in that place and burn the books. In those places the people that were left weren't abreast to the history of their nation because of what colonialist and imperialists did to the motherland.

This wasn't the case with Ethiopia. Ethiopia still had its history preserved and up until the 20th or 21st century it existed on an "island" free of outsiders. It wasn't until Haile Selassie I became emperor that the gates of Ethiopia were opened and He had a lot of the ancient texts converted into different languages that we had access to the history that we have today.

My problem with a lot of the movements that I was apart of was always in the leadership. Not necessarily saying that I had problems with people in the leadership, but more so the policies and directions that the leaders were choosing to go that disturbed me. I'm thankful for all of the experiences that I received through these learning cycles and avenues in my life and without those insights and experiences, I wouldn't be able to do what I'm doing today with the program Visionary Leaders of Society.

I came up with concept in 2016. At the time it was just a movement to unite the Vice Lords, mainly the ones that were righteous or on the path to righteousness. It was a means to become involved with our community and get away from the negative stigma of being a Vice Lord. I didn't have the vision back then that I have now.

After filling my mind with the research and information, in the year 2018…I was able to draft a more concrete and solid plan to further carry out this movement of Visionary Leaders. I feel like in the future, this will be a force to be reckoned with. I want the ones that come up under the leadership of the program to embrace it as the same.

Ultimately, my take on presentation is this. Anytime you are presenting or letting people see what you have going on, we've got to remember that quality is key. When ones see the blueprint and they respect the blueprint of what you have to offer…the whole process with go smoother and fulfilling to the cause of that program. That being said…we've got to always remember the packaging of anything is important. Even looking at yourself, because at the end of the day we are a package.

Not saying that we should treat ourselves as anything less. The body is indeed the temple and anything that we let in that means us harm, will be detrimental to the whole body and to be honest…we don't want that. That is a hindrance in our growth.

Epilogue...

I would like to thank you for taking the time to allow me to share my story and knowledge with you. As we stated earlier, this is P.I.M.P, Perception, Influence, Marketing and Presentation. I definitely hope you enjoyed this.

Currently in my life, I'm building multiple businesses and what I plan to do is to continue to educate our people in the economics, the history, the literary and also in the spiritual to inspire growth both individually and as a whole. I feel in our community, we lack organization, we lack leadership and we lack the discipline to do what we need to do.

I'm sharing my story with you to give you a glimpse of my life so that you get an understanding of what humbled me to make the choices that I made to be on the path that I am on. I'll continue to remain strong, steadfast and hungry for what's instore for me and I would like you to do the same.

Until we meet again...Love, Truth, Peace, Freedom and Justice.

ALMIGHTY.

www.ingramcontent.com/pod-product-compliance
Lightning Source LLC
Chambersburg PA
CBHW030540220526
45463CB00007B/2916